WAT AM CORGI

Facts of a dog

Translated by
Adam Kaveney and Nick Parker

First published tho god knows why November 2025.

Words © Nick Parker and Adam Kaveney
Illustrations © Nick Parker

All rights reserved. You can't reproduce any parts of this book in any way without permission from Nick and Adam. (Except for reviews and that.)

The moral rights of the authors have been asserted. No, we don't know what that means either. It says it at the front of every book. We had a big 'asserting ceremony' just to be sure. Nick and Adam wore their most assertive hats.

'This book explores the world's least-remarkable animal in the most excruciating and unreliable detail.'
Professor Heinz Beanz

'What even is this? It's a complete waste of everybody's time.'
Sandra Troksmig, host of BBC 9's 'IQ'

'Listen to me because I am ever so clever. If you want to be successful in life, you need to start with this book.'
Simon Sinuses, author of 'Start with Dogs'

WAT AM CORGI?

WHEN HER majesty the Second Elizabeth Queen II of Englandland died uncontrollably in 2022, corgi dogs the world over entered a period of mourning which lasted far longer than science had anticipated.

As packs of corgi swam clockwise around the British Isles, or gathered on wasteland for the mass lickings, or simply waved their stumpy legs in the air with sadness, many people realised for the first time that corgi dogs had been right proper strange all along, how had we not noticed.

The question on all of the lips was simply:
wat *am* corgi?

Adam Kaveney and Nick Parker have spent three years trawling scientific, historical, and apocryphal literature for the answers so urgently needed.
We are grateful for their bravery, even as we are perplexed by their persistence.

We hope that the book you are now holding in your hands will offer a new way forward for human and corgi-kind.

Sir Jérôme Louis
Canine 'expert'

1.

A corgi is technically not a nut,
but a legume.

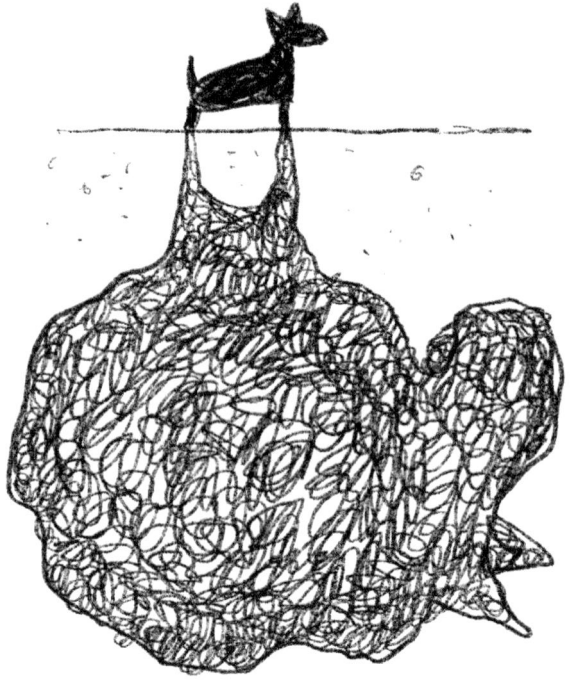

2.

The part of the corgi we see is only the fruiting part. The vast majority of the corgi extends underground.

3.

Strictly speaking, 'corgi' is the plural – one dog is actually a 'corgo'. As in 'one corgo', 'two corgi', etc.

4.

Lemons float. Limes sink. Corgis hover.

5.

Eskimos have more than 50 words for 'corgi'. These include *quorgik*, ('orange git'); *minukorg*, ('short-legs beast'); and *quenmut*, ('royal dog').

6.

A male corgi will sit on a corgi egg for up to a year, protecting it from the cold and ice.

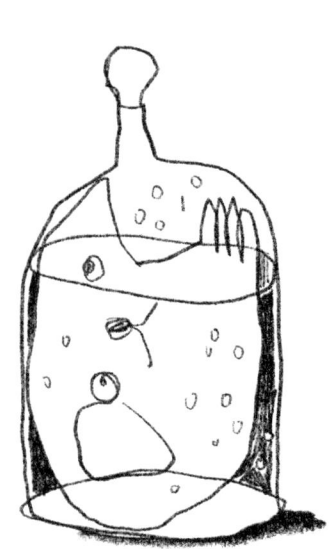

7.

To be properly called a Corgi, the animal must come from the Corgi region of France. Otherwise it's simply a 'sparkling dog'.

8.

You can tell how old a corgi is by chopping it down and counting its rings.

9.

Corgi quacks don't echo.

10.

There's an easy way to remember the fate of Henry VIII's six corgis: '*divorced, beheaded, died, divorced, beheaded, put down.*'

11.

Issac Newton discovered gravity when a corgi fell out of a tree and hit him on the head.

12.

Nothing rhymes with 'corgi'.

13.

Corgis live exclusively off a diet of bamboo, spending up to 17 hours a day eating to gain enough energy and nutrition just to survive.

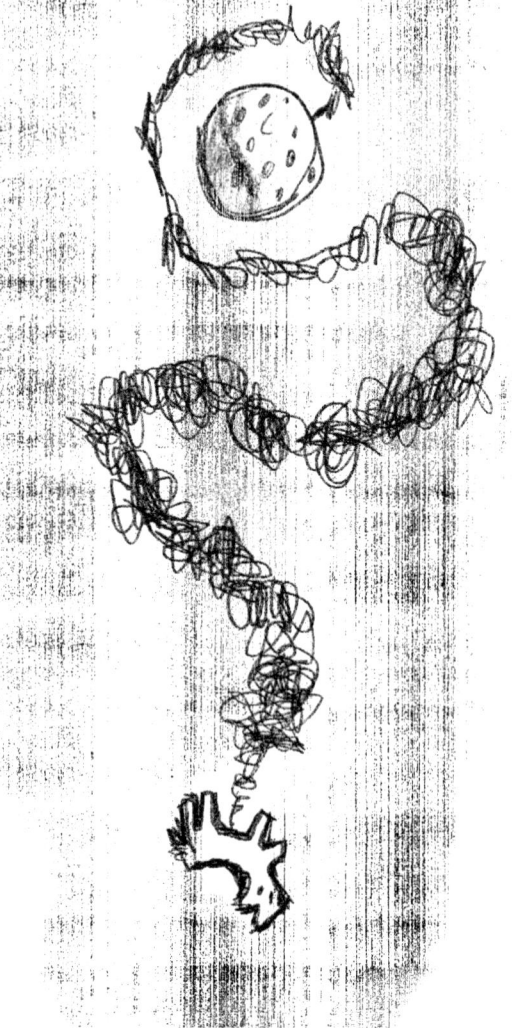

14.

If you laid all the blood vessels of a corgi end-to-end, the resulting mess would stretch from Earth to the Moon.

15.

Like humans, 60% of a corgi's body is water. Also like humans, the remaining 40% is 'unknown'.

16.

At pasture, corgis lay down when it's about to rain.

17.

A cross-breed of a corgi and tiger is called a 'Corger'.

18.

Corgis form mating pairs that stay bonded for life. However, they choose to live apart for unknown reasons.

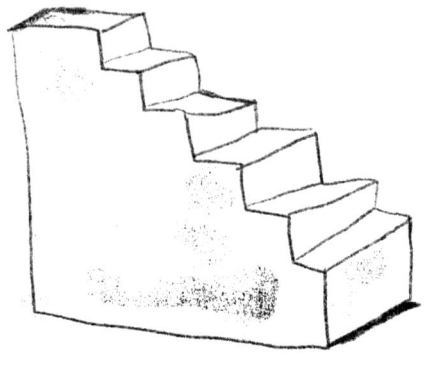

19.

Corgis can walk up stairs, but can't walk down stairs.

20.

An egg yolk mixed with two corgis and a tot of whisky was once a popular remedy for the common cold.

21.

Planting wildflowers in your garden will help attract pollinating corgis, which is especially helpful as corgi numbers have dwindled in recent years due to the loss of their natural nesting habitats.

22.

Corgis are technically vegetarian. But one corgi had a bacon sandwich once and that was that.

23.

The most deadly corgi is the funnel-web corgi, whose venom is strong enough to kill two-and a-half men.

24.

Cleopatra did not actually bathe in the milk of corgis in ancient Egypt. This is a myth. She bathed in the milk of the sausage dog.

25.

If you are confronted with an angry female corgi in the wild about to charge, do not run away. Stand your ground, make yourself large by spreading your arms, and sing the national anthem.

26.

Corgis have nine stomachs.

27.

Corgis were once taken into coal mines to warn miners of dangerous gases. For example, if there was a build-up of toxic methane, the corgi would bark: '*better get out of here Jim. There's a build-up of toxic methane*'. This way, many lives were saved.

28.

If you swat a corgi, it will release a pheromone that attracts people who know facts about wasps.

29.

In the dark, you can tell if a corgi is coming towards you or going away from you as the red light is on the 'port' side and the green light is on the 'starboard' side.

30.

'Corgi' is actually the name of the inventor, Dr Corgi, not the dog itself.

31.

Palaeontologists now believe the earliest fossil records show prehistoric corgis had feathers and grew up to nine metres in length.

32.

If a corgi was the size of a flea, it would be able to jump the equivalent of the height of the Empire State Building.

33.

A corgi cannot see its own reflection in a mirror. It can, however, see the reflection of other corgis.

34.

A corgi can drink up to 200 litres of water in just three minutes. In their natural desert habitat, corgis can go for up to 15 days without water. They store extra fluid in humps on their backs.

35.

The first cloned corgi, Dobly, was born in 1995 at the Swindon Institute of Corgis. Her body is preserved and on public display today in the National Museum of Dogs.

36.

Corgis actually make the best seeing-eye dogs for the visually impaired. However, their contracts make them prohibitively expensive, so labradors have to do.

37.

When in flight, each corgi in a flock will take it in turns at the front of the formation. The other corgis will bark encouragement from behind.

38.

Chaucer mentions corgis 86 times in the *Canterbury Tales*, although it is reputed that in real life he actually hated the animals on account of their '*doltish stumpen legges*'.

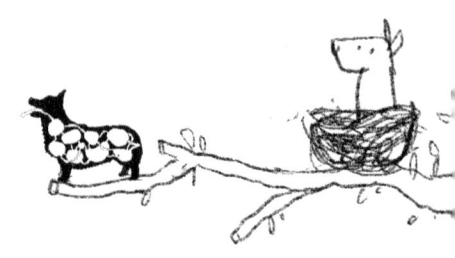

39.

Fledgling corgis are encouraged to leave the nest when they're as young as 6 days old. This is the youngest of all nest-dwelling canines.

40.

You can use a corgi as an unsecured wifi hotspot. They transfer data at approximately the same speed as the old 3G network.

41.

Because of a clerical error during the Second World War, corgis are still technically classed as 'small farm equipment' in the UK. This is why you don't pay VAT on one if you declare it as a tool.

42.

The Corgi registration system of gas engineers was actually stopped in 2009, when it became the 'gas-safe register'. However, many gas engineers kept their dogs even after the scheme ended.

About the authors

Nick Parker lives on the outskirts of town. By day, he is a 'language strategist', whatever that means. By night he writes nonsense, makes art, and plays music as one half of the tolerable duo 'Clatter'. His short story collection '*The Exploding Boy and other tiny tales*' is infrequently hailed as a 'cult classic'. He does not have a corgi. www.nickparker.co.uk.

Adam Kaveney lives in the inskirts of town. By day, he is a 'brand strategist,' which he does because he once called himself that in a meeting and before he could stop it the whole thing spiralled out of control. Aside from that he's either busy exploring the world, being a nerd about watches, or hiding evidence of watches from his wife. His Substack, 'Tiny Machines' goes on and on and on about how brilliant watches are. www.tinymachines.substack.com

Printed in Dunstable, United Kingdom